Introduction

The Castle Market in Sheffield has a place in many peoples' hearts. In thi[s] special about the market on the eve of its move from Exchange Street to

This work was generated as part of a community project called *Trading Histories*. [Ri]ch[...] photographers and poets worked with volunteers and the traders to document the market and explore its history, its people and their memories. The project ran from November 2012 to October 2013, covering the final year of the market at its location in Exchange Street prior to its move to new premises on The Moor.

Do you remember buying sweet fishes? Did you ever get a shirt from Harringtons? Did you jump on the weighing scales as a child? And what about the remains of Sheffield Castle, lurking in the ground below...

NO! BONES

Quality
GUARANTEED

MAR K...

Ladies
Fashion

Bags

Shoes

Jewellery

Accessori...

O M G...

Sheffield
Pensioners
Action Group
on gallery →

Cafe Open
Mon - Sat
home made dinners
O.A.P Specials
Upstairs

image: Ian Beesley

ii

Menu

image: Hannah Baxter

Market Charters

A poem by Ian McMillan, Laura Alston, Hannah Baxter, Steve Bush, Moira Campbell, Pam Courtenay, T. Davies, David Harpham, Stephen Harpham, Sue Harpham and Vibecke Yrstad

My dream is of a market
A market full of gold
Ready Steady – Start it!
Keep the stories that we've told
Even though it's going
The tales just keep on growing

Charters are a marker
Holding all the rules
Accumulating data
Reaching wise folk, reaching fools
Tell it to the masses
Everlasting as time passes
Round the castle, take a tour
Stroll up Fargate, down the Moor!

Market Charter

The Original Charter of 1296

Know ye that we have granted and by this charter have confirmed to our beloved and faithful Thomas de Furnyvall that he and his heirs for ever may have one market in every week on Wednesday at his Manor of Wyrkesop in the county of Nottingham, and one fair there in every year to last 8 days, that is to say, on the eve and on the day and on the morrow of St. Cuthbert the Bishop (March 20th) and for the 5 days following and one market in every week on Tuesday at his manor of Sheffield in the county of York. And one fair there in every year to last for three days, that is to say, on the eve and on the day and on the morrow of the Holy Trinity, unless those markets and fairs be to the nuisance of neighbouring markets and fairs. And that they may have free warren in all their desmense lands of Wyrkesop in the aforesaid county of Nottingham and in all their desmense lands of Sheffield in the aforesaid county of York. Provided that the same lands be not within the metes of our Forest, so that no one may enter those lands to chase in them or to take anything which appertains to the warren without the license and will of the same Thomas or his heirs upon forfeiture to us of £10. Wherefore we will and firmly enjoin for ourselves and our heirs that the aforesaid Thomas and his heirs for ever may have the aforesaid markets and fairs, unless those markets and fairs be to the injury of neighbouring markets and fairs. And that they may have free warren in all their desmense lands aforesaid, so long however, as those lands be not within the metes of our forest so that no one may enter those lands to hunt in them or to take anything which pertains to the warren without the license and will of the said Thomas or his heirs, under forfeiture to us of ten pounds is aforesaid.

Those being witnesses, the Venerable Fathers A. Bishop of Durham, W. Bishop of Ely, and W. Bishop of Bath and Wells, Roger le Bygod Earl of Norfolk and Marshal of England, Humfry de Bohun Earl of Hereford and Essex, Hugh le Despenser, Reginald de Grey, John Wake, Robert Fitz Roger, John de Hastanges, Robert de Tateshall, Peter de Chauvent, Peter de Patyngton and others.

Given by the hand of the King at St. Edmund's, the 12th day of November (1296)

Atmosphere

The Castle Market is a lively, bustling place full of friendly people, colour, smells and noise.

'I love when you go into the fish and meat market, I love the smells and they attack your senses right away, a little bit overpowering if you're not used to it. You could almost still smell the sea on these fish.'

Steve Bush

'Calling out 'Buy here! Buy there!' 'Over here this is the cheapest stall on the market!' Someone else would say 'Ours is better quality' or 'We give you your change' - you can join in with the fun, you know? It certainly weren't miserable. Good Yorkshire fun!'

Joan Hanley Read

'People being friendly I guess, no pushing and shoving but if there was, always a sorry or an excuse me.'

Ron Gutteridge

'There's people who are probably a bit less fortunate but they've always been well looked after here, we've always taken them under our wing, looked after them, they've eaten for free, you know, you can see them going home with lots of shopping for free from the traders, people are really, really well looked after, everybody was welcome.'

Nikolas Erodotou

'It were so busy. It were the noise, the chatter, the atmosphere, if felt as though all Sheffield were here, particularly on busy days. There were just everything, everything you could want, you didn't need to go anywhere else. To me it were heart of Sheffield.'

Nora Platt

SALE

image: Ian Beesley

image: Ian Beesley

Cheap Very good **Welcoming** Fish
Crozzled bacon Wet floor Love
Tea Sheffield people Pleasantly
pleasing Broken biscuits Colourful
Fully stocked Joe Bloggs jeans
Trendy style Community Toasted
teacake Sausage sarnies Sweets
Obliging Friendly Mussels Iconic
Tripe in vinegar Effervescent

6

Garden Eggs and Steam Bananas

A poem created using phrases overheard, seen and collected in the Castle Market on 11th December 2012 by Ian McMillan, Hannah Baxter, Suzannah Evans and Kate Rutter

Two pigs heads in a cardboard box
Opposite the nut bar
You've got to look for the positive
He said, dividing the ribs of an enormous animal
If you like Marc Jacobs Daisy try this

Two pigs heads in a cardboard box
Opposite the nut bar

Every clock shows a different time
Wood stamps – handled all at half price
From me to you with deepest sympathy
Please do not mix green, yellow, red, and so on
Various toasties, various omelettes

Two pigs heads in a cardboard box
Opposite the nut bar

Padded shirts
Undressed dollies 1.29 with shoes
Father's Day June 27th, Don't forget
Garden eggs

Two pigs heads in a cardboard box
Opposite the nut bar

Strangers in the night
How much is it – I never asked
The Seventh Direction, this way
Look fishy Ian is trying to catch us again

Two pigs heads in a cardboard box
Opposite the nut bar

QUALITY PRODUCT

I used to visit Sheffield Markets regularly with my Nan-Nan (Lillian Bennett) ~ Castle Market, Sheaf Market and the outdoor markets in-between.

Outdoors, I liked the rummagey bric-a-brac stalls where Nan-Nan once bought me a cute little hand-operated sewing machine.

I still have this vintage 1950s machine to this day →

image: Missy Tassles

Childhood

Many memories shared in the market are of childhood, of families, growing up and exploring the wider world. Experiences that shape who we are.

'The old lady with the big weighing scales in the doorway. Big brass they were with a red seat. And buying my fishes and me marry-me-quick which you couldn't get anywhere else. And Potty Edwards selling his pots and Harry, Larry and Mo the three Jewish gentlemen who had a material stall. And there was an awful lot you could buy from them that you couldn't get anywhere else.'

Elizabeth Aizlewood, Rag and Tag in the 1940s

'Potty Edwards was fantastic! He'd got a fan of plates in his hand and then he would throw them up in the air and as they'd drop down he'd catch them and they'd still all stay together and he'd say 'Now ladies, I'm not just giving you the plates, we've got a cup and a saucer, in fact we've got six cups and saucers!' And they'd all go on and then he'd throw it up and then you'd hear them ching. And I used to think 'He'll drop it, he'll drop it!' And he never, ever did.'

Betty Smith, Rag and Tag in the 1940s

'I remembered this chair that looked like a throne and this, what seemed to be an old lady, maybe she weren't so old when I look back, but I think you used to pay her a couple of pennies or whatever and it used to weigh you. And everyone used to queue up to go on it, or they used to look at it longingly if they couldn't'.

Nora Platt, Rag and Tag in the 1950s

'I remember the Turner's tool stall, cos I'd just started putting a bit of tool kit together, for mending my trolley and me bike and things like that, bits and pieces at Turner's tool shop. And then there's misty memories of somebody who used to do sort of medicine type things, I suppose it'd be herbal remedies that'd cure everything - all of everything!'

Peter Courtenay, Rag and Tag in the 1950s

Childhood

'We were very short of money. It didn't cost anything to go on a tram if you were under five so me mum used to put me on the tram at the bottom of Granville Road, I used to get off near the market near Commercial Street, walk through to the Rag and Tag market and then I used to have to knock on the counter of the little shop - Bingham's it was - and I used to hand them my list of food that we wanted to buy and then they'd put it me all in a little bag and then I'd get back on the tram and me mum would be waiting for me at the other end.'

George Buckley, Rag and Tag in the 1950s

'My mum used to leave me with one of the stallholders that she knew and he used to sit me on a little stool behind out the way and I'd have a little book and just sit and crayon until she did all her shopping and then came back and collected me'.

Linda Cardwell, Castle Market in the 1960s

'We would walk into town, and that's about four miles from where I live, you know? We walked everywhere. We'd only get the bus back with the shopping bags. And there are a lot of things, just images of colour and bustle, and the flavours, you know the flavours of the fish and the greasy chips, and the sweet tea, and the custard tarts, that we had here'.

Sian Podmore, Castle Market in the 1960s

image: Ian Beesley

Castle Market

John Burkhill

Castle Market oh what a place
Home to everyone no matter what colour creed or race
Where you could buy anything at the blink of an eye
And when the shopping was finished a lovely pork pie

The market is somewhere you can chat and have a fag
As you recall the memories and the old Rag and Tag
Potty Edwards who threw his plates high never broke one on that you can bet
For when they came down it was a wonderful tea set

Then there was Pete who sold everything even a spanner
And guess your weight Edna who if she got it wrong would give you a tanner
Yes the market was top of the tree
The ideal place for me and thee

Down in the fish market you can get any fish you can name
Buy it somewhere else it never tastes the same
Getting served you don't have to stand round a while
And you always get a welcome and friendly smile

All Sheffield will miss the lads and lasses they were the best
The best market better than all the rest
Thanks for the memories 74 years they will live with me forever
Remembering you yes forgetting you never

Thanks so much 'The Mad Man with the Pram' John

image: Ian Beesley

image: Samantha Galbraith

Treats

Trips to the market could be a time for treats - sandwiches, tea, shellfish, biscuits and sweets – an opportunity for small indulgences

'One thing that sticks in my mind is that it was probably the first place that we ever ate out, that is, not eating in house, buying a sandwich and actually sitting in a café'.

Ron Gutteridge

'Me dad would have whelks, I'd have cockles and then we'd probably buy some prawns and sit upstairs in the front of the tram, I remember that, pullin' the heads and legs and tails off the prawns and eating them on the way home.'

Ted Evans

'Mum would do her shopping, buy lots of her fruit here and things like that. And I always remember, whenever she'd finished her shopping we used to go and have a cup of - well we called it a cup of tea stood up, because there were no seats we just went to the counter - and so we would have a cup of tea'.

Steve Bush

'There were all the different sweet shops and the broken biscuit shop, where you used to go in and say 'Mam, can I have some broken biscuits?' and you'd go to the counter and the lady would say 'Oh I haven't got any today' and then she'd just smash a few up and make sure that you got some'.

Judd Newton Cutts

'The sugared fish were about three inches long and we used to delight in holding them by the tail and sucking them until the outer pattern came off and then the inner hard sugar part was clear and sparkly and you could hold it up and see the sun through it. And I absolutely loved those and that was an absolute luxury of a treat, for us, to have those sweets.'

Betty Smith

Moira's Market Morning

A poem by Ian McMillan and Moira Campbell

Moira Campbell was originally from Liverpool but moved to Sheffield with her husband when they got married. She had never shopped in a market like the Castle Market before but her mother-in-law taught her how. A mortgage on her first house meant she had to be careful, but it was difficult not to be tempted by the sweet stalls.

I was trying to walk past the Acid Drop stall
For cheaper meat at t'other end
I didn't know what "Gee'or" meant
But I've a little money to spend
We feel as if we're floating rich
Tempted by some tripe
I couldn't find the butcher's pitch
But the fruit was really ripe
Now it's time for a cuppa
At Sallie's, and a bun
Then I'll buy a stuffed cat
A mousetrap, then I'm done

image: Ian Beesley

The very first time I ever went into town without an adult, aged about 11, it was to Castle Market. I was allowed to go with my friend Sarah (who had been into town without parents before), and we went to the market as the bus stopped nearby, and it was somewhere I was already familiar with. I wasn't especially nervous or excited but it felt a bit odd I remember. The other main thing I recall is buying a long bendy yellow pencil from a party stall!

image: Missy Tassles

Growing Up

Traders and shoppers have grown up in the market, learning skills from their mothers and fathers and bringing their own children to teach them in turn

'A lot of us worked there for a number of years so we grew up together, literally. We grew up together over twenty five years and we went from all young men to having our own families, taking over from either their fathers or uncles. So I mean it was a community within a community'.

Ian Spooner, Harringtons

'I started working Saturdays when I was 14, so we're going what roughly 30 years? It was sort of my first experience of work at all, it was really, really, really packed, fantastic sort of sense of community amongst the traders and the staff - like its own little ecosystem. It was completely separate to anything I'd ever experienced before. It was my father's business and now it's been passed on to me. So he was a cobbler and his father before him was a cobbler. My grandfather was a cobbler in Cyprus'.

Nikolas Erodotou, Happy Feet

'My favourite memory of the market here was in about 1967-68 when I was just at secondary school and I was starting to think about fashion in a way that I never had done before. And there was a shop in the market here called Harringtons and there was a style of popular jacket at that time called the Harrington, and purely by coincidence Harringtons sold Harringtons and I came in, and I tried two or three on with me mum and it was a toss-up between a black one and a Prince of Wales check jacket, and I ended up getting the Prince of Wales check, and I thought I looked the bees knees in it'.

Steve Bush

SINCE
1959

image: Kid Acne

image: Ian Beesley

Growing Up

'My mother sewed for me all my life, and by the time I got to the age of fourteen I was a dab hand with the sewing machine and then when my children came I sewed for them and went to Harry, Larry and Mo. My grandma and my mum and I always bought our material from them and particularly at Whitsuntide when they bought their material and made their outfits for the Whitsuntide parade, on Whit Monday when they followed the Sunday School banner. And when we'd made the outfits then we went off and took them down when the kids were all dressed up to see Harry, Larry and Mo'.

Elizabeth Aizlewood

'My mother used to buy curtain fabric. She used to buy fabric to make dresses, for myself when I was a small child but then, as I got older and got my own house and my own family I used to buy fabric from the market and I gave my children the choice of colours they wanted in their rooms. My son wanted black and white in his bedroom. I went into the market and there was a stall that used to sell the roll ends of the fabric and it was a designer fabric that had been very, very expensive and it was white background with this beautiful black pattern on it and I made a pair of curtains and a bedcover and they are still in my son's bedroom since 1976.'

Betty Smith

'I worked on it when it was built. I was an apprentice for William Moss and Sons from Loughborough, and they built this newest section to the Castle Market. It was a brilliant experience. I was perhaps 18 years old. You know it was a real good experience for someone of my age, I suppose I thought I was Jack the Lad at that time.'

Judd Newton Cutts

'I can remember when I'd got young children I used to bring them in the market on a Saturday morning. I used to love taking them, just to get the feel of what it used to be like in the old days, so I'd take them to the tripe shop, and we'd get a little plate of tripe or a plate of mussels or cockles or something like that. They used to love it.'

George Buckley

image: Ian Beesley

Castle Market

A poem by Suzannah Evans

You've got to look for the positive he says,
dividing the ribs of an enormous animal
cleaver-swing, broken branch crack. He's better off
without her says Graham behind the counter
laying out brisket and cling-filmed liver
his trilby a hygienic white. Better in the long run
says the woman at the till, slips her carrier bag
into her other hand, proffers a fiver.

The market has reduced to this last circle;
butchers, nut bar, Chinese supermarket. Downstairs
they're boarding up and going, more each day.
The card stall is long gone; the sign reads
FATHERS DAY 27TH JUNE (DON'T FORGET!)

But it's December now and on the other side of town
a new market is rising like under tarpaulins
sticking out girdered knees and elbows to push up a roof.
They've cut windows in the temporary fencing
so we can watch the crane drivers and stare
into the cemented gape of its foundations.

MADE
FRESH
DAILY

BROKEN
CONSOLE?

99p

image: Ian Beesley

Shopping

A market is for shopping for food, clothes, electrical goods, tools - almost anything was available in Castle Market

'My son ended up being six foot five tall and he'd got a thirty-six inch inside leg and I struggled to buy clothes for him and he was like his dad, he hated clothes shopping. And once I brought him into here because Harringtons had a sign up saying 'Big Shirts for Big Men' or something. And we went in and he chose some shirts that he wanted and they said 'Oh don't worry. We can always get you the 19 inch shirts.' And we said, 'What about the jeans?' And they used to look out for the jeans for me. And then when my son had finished at college and university he went out to America. And they thought he would be able to buy the big clothes in America. And unfortunately in Arizona he couldn't, and he used to phone me up and say, 'Mother, go to that stall in Castle Market and get me some shirts.'

Betty Smith

'All Seasons Fruit and Veg, is the best fruit and veg shop in Sheffield by my mind. And Simmo's, we always go to Simmo's the butcher, I get all us meat from Simmo, and usually I have a ten minute chat with him and he's great cos he just takes the Mickey out of everybody and it's always good fun. We regularly come in and go to Sallie's on Saturday morning and I'll have a bacon sandwich, and just sit and enjoy talking to people. There is a kind of community to shopping in the market that doesn't really exist in other types of high street shops.'

Steve Bush

'Always get what I want there; fresh salmon, finny haddock, buy eggs from them, or chickens, bit of chicken. And then there's a guy, at Wateralls, go there and get some lovely big gammon steaks, you get two whacking gammon steaks for about a fiver and they'll do two people, two days. Some really quality stuff.'

Ted Evans

image: Ian Beesley

WATCHES
BATTERIES
&
STRAPS
FITTED
HERE

Shopping

'I come to have keys cut for church because that's the best place to have them done, round the corner. I come for my meat and for my vegetables because there's one of the stalls that sells pork and they dip it and I don't know if you've had pork that's been dipped but it turns to a beautiful pink colour when it's cooked and it makes a difference.'

Elizabeth Aizlewood

'I still come because the meat market is very good and fresh fish and yeah, I still come on average about once a week and sometimes I stop on my way over from work in the week. But it's just a nice family atmosphere, really nice. You tend to have your own old favourites that you've always gone to, especially if my Mum went to them.'

Linda Cardwell

Shopping List
Meat
Vegetables
Bread
Milk
Cleaning products
Handbag
Bulbs
Newspaper
Fruit
Scones
Dog chews
Coffee
Electric fan
Back pack
Breadcakes
Shoulder pads
Pork pie
Yorkshire pudding

Chicken
Lamb
Butter
Bird seed
Flowers
Bananas
Rat poison
Brass curtain hooks
Knitting needles
Curtains
Kitchen roll
Fish and chips
Yellow yarn
Sticky mouse pads
Newspaper
Chocolate
Fish
Cigarettes

Nuts
Grapes
Cheese
Buttons
Zip
Shallots
Tomatoes
Spring onions
Cherry tomatoes
Mushrooms
Bedsocks
Parkin
Cards
Tea towel holder
Roasty dog bones
Black pudding
Sausage
Duck eggs

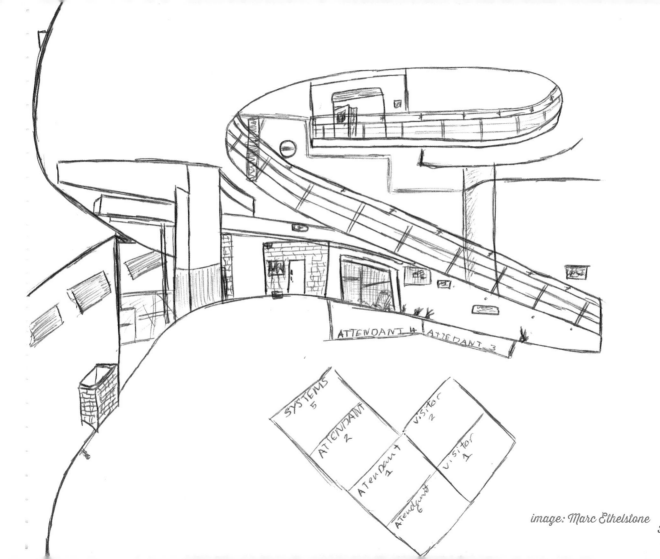

ATTENDANT 4   ATTENDANT 3

SYSTEMS 5	VISITOR 2	
ATTENDANT 2	Attendant 1	Visitor 1
	Attendant 6	

image: Marc Ethelstone

32

John Colley, JC Books

John Colley owns JC Books with his wife Helen. He has worked in Sheffield markets since he was a boy. Here is John's story.

My grandfather had a shop on Scotland Street, which was a lot of Jewish traders, selling all the nylons, and nightdresses, and towels. We were surrounded by old Jewish traders which we became very friendly with. And that would be the 40s and 50s when I was just a nipper.

My father was one of three sons and the other two went into the steelworks and my father was the one who carried on with the business from his father. I helped my father as soon as I was independent enough to come down from school. The old Rag and Tag was outdoors and in the winter my father could hardly walk home after the cold - terrible stood all day in the open air in the cold. So we used to go to the nearest pub which was on Dixon Lane and my father had to have a hot barley wine before we walked to the bus stop to catch the bus home.

We had a little warehouse which was at the side of the pet shop, the big pet shop Oggleys, and we used to have to pack the books away off the stall every night into these boxes, push them down into our warehouse, lock the warehouse up and go home. We'd come early in the morning, unlock the warehouse and push the boxes back up to the stall. The council market workers would then put you two trestles up and wooden planks across the top and you displayed the stall how you thought appropriate.

In those days my father had to go up on the train to the wholesale to buy the stuff - Manchester and Leeds, especially Manchester. Things started to change then after the 50s when we got our first car, a little Morris Minor, and then we could bring a little more stuff down. My father died suddenly at the age of 64, I was in my 20s. So I took over, and it wasn't too long before then we were transferred to the Sheaf which was an entirely different set up, that became a five day market (the Rag and Tag was only open Tuesday, Friday and Saturday). And it's been that way ever since.

The times have changed now but we used to sell lots and lots of colouring books and at Christmas time the big input was the Christmas Annuals, which in those days was Dandy and Beano and Bunty. Comics were one of our biggest lines, the old American comics, which I wish I'd have kept hold of some of them cos they'd be worth a fortune nowadays, the early Superman and Batman American comics, Marvel comics, we used to sell hundreds a week of those American comics.

If I remember correctly the only time we ever had a queue waiting to be served at my stall was for the output of Lady Chatterley's Lover, which was the Penguin paperback which caused such a reaction, and that was the only time we've ever had a queue. I think it must have sold almost a hundred on the very first day of publication and it was, I can remember, in the old Penguin orange and white covers and I'm sure it was priced either 2/6 or 3/6, I think it was 3 shillings and sixpence. That was a long time ago.

Lots and lots of people will remember us from the day they started bringing pop magazines out. Things like the Beatles Monthly and Rolling Stones magazines, and Donny Osmond's, the Osmonds, and they used to open out some of them into photos of Donny Osmond, etc. and I used to pin them up open behind the stall and we sold lots and lots of those - Donny Osmond, David Cassidy, the Beatles, David Bowie, David Essex and perhaps the biggest of all was the Bruce Lee karate/kung-fu magazines which I used to sell possibly 200 plus a month. That was the real craze in those days. One year all the young girls were queuing at the City Hall up town for tickets to see the Bay City Rollers, which were the current craze and luckily on that weekend I had a Bay City Roller magazine that opened out into a giant picture of the pop group so first thing in the morning the tickets went on sale and all the girls heard that there was a picture for sale in a magazine down at the market and I was inundated by school girls buying this magazine. I sold out in less than two hours of the Bay City Rollers. So ever since then I've been a Bay City Rollers fan.

At that time we were in the Sheaf. Then the Sheaf market began to be run down and they began to move us all into one place for the convenience. We were moved across to share this Castle Market building which will be about the late 1990s. We came across here and we've been here ever since.

Things changed when I got married, I married the wife in 1980. And she packed her job up and came into the market with me, and she really has kept the business going because I think most of the people who read are women, women tend to read, and so she's been able to chit chat more and being a big reader herself it became an interest as a hobby - still the most popular being the old Mills and Boons, romance and the Catherine Cookson type books. She won the shopkeeper personality of the year just a few years back with her photo in the local Star and the interviews and I think that the business is still going is entirely due to my wife and daughter. Nowadays, being 70, I'm still taking a backseat, I do the invoices and the office work.

We shall just have to see how this new market goes - or they will just have to see how this market goes! But I'm sure being so good at the job and knowing books as they do I feel confident they'll make a success of it.

Extracts from 'Bye laws'

By The Lord Mayor, Aldermen and Citizens of the City of Sheffield. The Minister of Housing and Local Goverment. 6th October 1954 and 4th October 1956.

(8) Cleaving. No person shall in any Market place, cleave any carcase or meat unless it is upon a cleaving block or chopping board, or properly attached to or suspended from hooks provided for the purpose.

(16) No person shall cause obstruction or annoyance in any market place or its immediate approaches - (a) by touting or hawking goods for sale, or (b) by using the market for purposes which are not related to the buying or selling of goods.

(18) No person shall wilfully throw or drop any waste fruit or vegetable matter or any other market litter in or upon any avenue, or passage in any market place, or upon the staircases in the Castle Market in a manner likely to cause injury to any person.

(19) No person shall wilfully throw or drop any object whatsoever into the apertures provided for the purpose of ventilation and lighting in the upper ground floor of the Castle Market in a manner likely to cause injury to any person, stall or goods.

(23) Crying for sale. No person shall cry any article whatsoever for sale in any market place or by ringing a bell or blowing any horn or by using any other noisy instrument seek to attract the attention or custom of any person to any stall or to any article or thing intended for sale; provided that this prohibition so far as it relates to crying shall not apply to the pitching stalls designated by the council within the Sheaf Market.

(24) No person shall pluck any poultry in any market place, other than the Castle Market and the Wholesale fish market.

(28) No person shall in any market place tout for or take an order for any marketable commodity not in such market place for which toll would be paid if the same had been offered for sale in such market place.

(30) No person shall throw any stone, brick, shell, cabbage leaf, garbage, offal or other matter or thing whatsoever except water into any fountain, water basin or grate of any market place.

(33) Every person who shall offend against any of the provisions of these byelaws shall on summary conviction be liable to a fine not exceeding the sum of five pounds.

image: Ian Beesley

36

Ian Spooner, Harringtons

Ian Spooner worked for Harringtons. He started as a Saturday lad and became the manager of the Harringtons shirt stall. Here is Ian's story.

I started as a Saturday lad, approximately 1971. I remember my first day because it was at the time of when Whit holidays meant that people bought new clothes. And it was the Saturday, the first Saturday I started. And I remember David Harrington's father-in-law, Claud, running me ragged as he was selling things, asking me to go and fetch them for him. Little did he know that it was my first day and I didn't know where to go for a lot of the things.

After a couple of weeks working as a Saturday lad, David Harrington offered me a full time job. He said that he actually wanted somebody to look after his stall when he wasn't there, because he came from Leeds and he was finding it very difficult to get down every day. So he saw me as someone who could manage his stall. He told me in no uncertain terms that if I was coming along just to serve and just be a shop worker that I was wasting my time and that he saw me as a manager and someone who potentially would buy stock, set prices and run the business for him. At first it was difficult for me and I had to prove myself so I was the one who did everything and if it needed doing I didn't ask anybody to do it, I did it myself and sort of led by example.

Harringtons was split into two sections; the upstairs stall was run by Brian Harrington, David Harrington's son, that predominantly sold trousers and jeans and the stall that I worked on specialised in shirts. We had our own shirts made. We also made made-to-measure shirts which was quite a daunting experience and something that I didn't enjoy because by nature a lot of the people who came for made-to-measure shirts were discerning customers and very difficult to please. We specialised in big sizes. We had a very small gap near where the fixtures were in our small stall and if somebody could get through that gap we knew that we could fit them up. On one occasion though, a customer came in and I judged that we could fit him up, I put the measure round his chest and it didn't meet - so that's a 60 inch tape measure, so for our 66 inch chest shirts to fit there needed to be some room - so I said in my opinion that shirt wouldn't fit. Then a customer came in the same day and I again felt confident we'd be able to fit them up and again I put the measure round the chest and it didn't meet again and it was only later in the day that I discovered that nine inches had fallen off the end of the tape measure and it wasn't actually 60 inches that I was measuring but 51 inches!

A lot of customers that I remember were the larger sized customers and one or two famous customers - Paul Shane the Barnsley actor and comedian who appeared on various television shows such as Hi-De-Hi - he was a customer of ours because he came for big sized clothing. But the person who springs to mind more than anything is a person called Brian Platts who was, I think, the founder and the leading light in the Manor Operatic Society and they do much loved Christmas performances in Sheffield. Now Brian was a very large person and he played the Dame in the pantomimes. He was a really nice chap and he used to come and buy quite a lot of clothing from us.

A lot of women bought for their husbands or boyfriends. Sometimes, you'd say 'Yes, what size would you like'? And they'd say 'Ooh I don't know!' Now how anybody could come shopping for a shirt and not know the size is beyond me! But I suppose that's the impulsive nature about shopping. On one occasion, famously, one of our customers actually said when asked what size shirt her husband was 'I don't know but he takes a nine in a shoe'!

Customers came to the stall because they trusted us, they knew that we'd do our best to give them a good service and good value. And out of loyalty you'd get customers coming back time and time again and that's what the business was built up on. In my opinion things have changed, society's changed, people go further afield for things now and I don't think you've got that local affinity with places anymore so I don't think you've got that loyalty anymore.

A lot of the skills I've got now were learnt from that market stall, and you know, the nearly twenty five years that I worked there have had a big influence on me as a person, my thoughts, my beliefs, and David Harrington had a big influence on my life. My father was very close to me but I was lucky because I'd got sort of a second father in David Harrington. One thing that David Harrington taught me above anything else was social justice and I think that's informed a lot of my adult beliefs about politics and social justice.

Closing

Sadness, and even anger, at the closing of the Castle Market demonstrates the affection with which it is held and its place in the lives of Sheffield people. But there is also hope for the new market on the Moor, that it will recapture the bustling atmosphere of a real Sheffield market.

'It's part of our heritage, you know what I mean? It's heartbreaking, not just for me but for a lot of Sheffielders, very, very hard, very hard.'

John Burkhill

'I'm hopeful that whatever they do, they do it well and I mean I think it will be funny it not being on this site, being up Moor. I know there's people want to preserve site of Sheffield castle, and I understand that cos I love history myself, but I just think maybe it've been better to have been on this site rather than up Moor. Because I think the Moor's got a different personality, hasn't it? So we'll see. It might bring life to the Moor, mightn't it?'

Nora Platt

'I didn't originally like the idea of the markets moving, I was kind of against that when it was first put out about twelve years ago. And I think one of the problems has been that the move just kept on being delayed and delayed. And now that the move is really taking place, and the new markets are being built, I am quite looking forward to seeing what the new markets will be like and hopefully to continue shopping there with some of the regular people.'

Steve Bush

'Excited? Nervous? It's a bit of a gamble isn't it? It's just about moving on to Moor Market and just hoping that people are gonna start embracing that and hopefully it will be a lot better than Castle Market's probably been. The Moor Market might be like Castle Market probably 20 year ago, you know with hustle and bustle hopefully. So we'll see.'

Jack Ruston

'700 years it's been here and now it's being moved? It'll take a bit of getting used to I think.'

Peter Courtenay

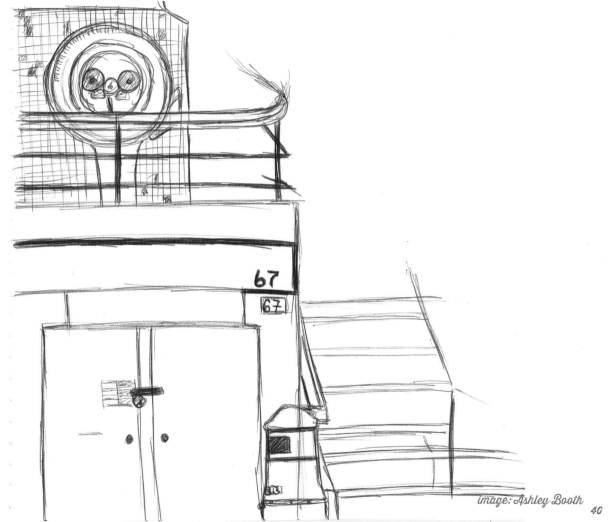

67

67

40

image: Samantha Galbraith

A Market Charter for 2013

"Eyup, it's fresh in 'ere!"

Nah then yore
Duz tha kno'
Thiz a market 'ere
Six days a week?

Nah then yore,
Eyup ah'r kid!
Breadcakes, teacakes,
'Alibut, cod.
Pooerk 'n ' aslet
Chicklin 'n' bag
Taters, caulies
Peyz 'n" sprouts
Knickers, booits
Cooerts 'n' 'ats
Bunnies 'n' budgies
Boooks 'n' biros
Endo's Relish
Owt tha wants
Carbolic Soo-erp? - Twenty-Seven Pence
Forever!
Forever?
Forever!!

These being witnesses:
Barbara Jones
Steve Bush
Hannah Baxter
Mark Sheridan
George Buckley
Pam Keally
Ian McMillan

The Fifteenth day of January (2013)

Genuine PRODUCT

42

Acknowledgements

The *Trading Histories* project was devised and managed by ArcHeritage (part of the York Archaeological Trust). We are indebted to the Heritage Lottery Fund for funding the project. Special thanks go to all the market traders for putting up with us, and to the volunteers who made the project happen. We are also very grateful to Andy Ward, Micheal Maloney and all Castle Market staff for allowing the project to take place and for great support throughout.

Thank you to Kid Acne, Bill Bevan, Tudur Davies (ArcHeritage), Tim Knebel (Sheffield Archives), Mark Johnson (York Archaeological Trust), Ian McMillan, Clara Morgan (Museums Sheffield), Jane Stockdale (York Archaeological Trust) and Robin Wiltshire (Sheffield Archives) for leading workshops.

Laura Alston, Hannah Baxter, Kirstin Baxter, Sharon Baxter, Richita Bhattacharyya, Laura Binns, Alicia Bonnington, George Buckley, John Burkhill, Steve Bush, John Buston, Moira Campbell, June Clegg, Pam Courtenay, Torri Crapper, T. Davies, Emily Elvin, Suzannah Evans, Helen Finnerty, Samantha Galbraith, David Harpham, Stephen Harpham, Sue Harpham, Thomas Heywood, Pam Keally, Shannon Kennedy, Debbie Mayor, Ian McMillan, Rosie O'Neill, Anna Parkinson, Kate Rutter, Mark Sheridan, Missy Tassles and Vibecke Ystadt contributed variously to archival research, oral history interviews, transcriptions, poetry and artwork.

A very special photographic record has been made by Ian Beesley.

Many of the above also took part in running six week-long stalls in the Castle Market to collect stories, along with Debra Baxter, Alex Fenton-Thomas, Olivia Froment, Mandy Holden, Barbara Jones, Brian Kershaw, Dennis Knight, Chris Kolonko, Jim Lambert, Joe Page, Penny Rea and Dorian Sheridan.

Design and layout by Gordon Webber, Snowgoose Promotions

VINTAGE QUALITY

Thank you to Simon Ogden, Yunus Ahmed and Matt Hayman of the City Regeneration Division for advice and support. Thank you also to Michael Auty (for the website design), Cheryl Bailey, Sarah Carpenter, Ron Clayton, Dee Desgranges, Michael Eden, Paulette Edwards, Graeme Hall, Nancy Fielder, Kim Marwood, Alex Migali, Laurence Peacock, Sarah Rawlins, Roni Robinson, Sally Rodgers, Chris Savage, Grace Tebbutt, Sue Wraith and Jayne Wright.

Finally, many more people told us their memories of the Castle Market than could possibly be included in this booklet. Our special thanks to:

Elizabeth Aizlewood, Kashif Ali Raja, Steve Bailey, Janet Barber, Debra Baxter, Mick Birks, Paul Brown, George Buckley, D. Burgayne, John Burkhill, Steve Bush, Linda Cardwell, Kath Clements, John Colley, Barbara Collins, Sandra Collins, Sean Collins, Charlene Collinson, Peter Courtenay, Anne Crossland, Fern Emmerson, Costas Erodotou, Nikolas Erodotou, Ted Evans, Alison Farr, Rita Fellows, John Farrell-Smith, J.R. Fearn, Anthony James Foulds, Ron Gutteridge, Joan Hanley Read, Norman Hardy, Lynsey Hunter, Royston Henry Jenkinson, Brian Kershaw, Dennis Knight, Alison Longden, Ms I. Marshall, Glen McDonell, Gail Morrison, Barry Nevin, Helen Newsome, Judd Newton-Cutts, Iria Oviasu, Mr and Mrs F. Parker, Frances Parker, Helen Parker, Lynn Parker, Janet Parkinson, Nora Platt, Sian Podmore, Lesley Pyatt, Penny Rea, Jack Ruston, John Savage, Michelle Simmons, Gordon Shephard, Mrs B. Smith, Paul Smith, Michael J. Staniforth, Simon Stewart, Steve Thompson, Alexandra Walker, M. Walker, Ted Watterson, Gordon Wildgoose, Maurice Wilkinson, John Whittaker, Jonathan and Susannah Youdan, Stephen Young and all who wished to remain anonymous.

Together these stories, artworks and images have created a wonderful record of the market which will be deposited in the Sheffield Archives. The material is also available on the project website: **www.sheffieldcastlemarket.co.uk**

image: Ian Beesley